THE
SOUL'S CALL
TO
AWAKENING

THE SPIRITUAL JOURNEY BACK TO SELF

WRITTEN AND CHANNELED BY
ISABEL MARTIN-VENTURA

To Johnny, THANK YOU.

Acknowledgements

I was once told that I am an old soul. And a slow learner. Thank you to spirit for its unending love and persistence.

Thank you, Lillian Scaglia, for your keen editing eye and enthusiasm.

AWAKE

To know the self is
essence true,
the reason for your life.

To meld the oneness that
is you
with the story now to
write.

To see within a grain of sand,
majesty alive.

To ride the wave of divinity
within the hands of time.

∞

TABLE OF CONTENTS

Introduction

There is a vitality, a life force, a quickening that is translated through you into action, and because there is only one of you in all time, this expression is unique. And if you block it, it will never exist through any other medium and be lost. The world will not have it. It is not your business to determine how good it is, nor how valuable it is, nor how it compares with other expressions. It is your business to keep it yours clearly and directly, to keep the channel open. You do not even have to believe in yourself or your work. You have to keep open and aware directly to the urges that motivate you. ~ Martha Graham

I don't know much about much, but what I do know is that there is a part of each and every one of us that is deep and rich and magical. There is an aspect of ourselves that is joyous and compassionate and knowing, and we spend a great deal of our lives trying to craft experiences that will give rise to this seemingly illusive facet of our being. We are called to connect and live from this place we can't quite define, but intuit exists. We are drawn to something that exists beyond our conscious knowing, yet we strive to touch the unknowable with the mind.

We search in relationships, work and accomplishments. We pursue meaning and purpose and even give ourselves the ultimate earthly challenge of changing the world. We falsely believe that if we try hard enough, we might be able to create something that will bring comfort from the gnawing feeling of emptiness, yet we find that regardless of what we have and do, eventually there is a return to wanting and needing more.

The truth is that nothing we do or have will fill the void. Nothing. It may falsely appear to do so for a while, but this is merely a distraction. When we respond to this inner call by attempting to create, we will eventually find that we are back to square one. When we search beyond ourselves to find what is within, when we strive in the quest to create stillness, we are only appeasing the mind. Eventually the mind will get distracted allowing the original yearning to break through the noise.

This yearning is not soothed by a random act of creation. It is only eased when we heed our soul's calling to remember our divine essence and live from the perspective of the true self. Our uneasiness arises from the disconnect between our divinity and our expression in the world. It is a question of misalignment one could say. When we choose to think and behave in ways that are out of alignment with our true nature, we feel broken. The only way to experience wholeness is through union. The journey of awakening is our experience of this process. Awakening simply means that we become aware of our divine essence and live its expression in our everyday lives.

The Soul's Call to Awakening is an offering. I have no thought on what it will become or what it will do for you. I am simply surrendering to my heart's call to put these words together and share them with the world.

My personal journey of spiritual unfolding has taken many turns, and in 2009 it took the form of channeling the written word, also known as automatic writing. In essence, I would get a sense to find a pen and paper to feverishly record the words that would start pouring into my mind. To help relate the experience, it was (and is) as if I was having a thought, yet I was aware that it was not my own. I could differentiate my own thoughts from what I was receiving. During the process, I would imagine what word or phrase might come next (I was never right). At times I would be unfamiliar with a word, writing it down phonetically until I could research the proper spelling and meaning. As I was writing the messages that were coming through, I would simultaneously be amazed, intrigued and inspired by the information. Within a minute or two, I would find before me one or more pages waiting to be read. I would consume the contents in their entirety, feeling overwhelmed and humbled by what was occurring.

Needless to say, this felt quite extraordinary. It's not every day that writings just "fall out of the sky." After the third day in a row, my husband just stared at me, and I knew exactly what he was thinking. "I'm not crazy," I responded to what his eyes were saying. Not too convinced, he asked "Are you sure?" I replied, "Yes. Yes, I am sure."

The writings continued over the course of one year. Speaking to the human condition and its connection to the Divine, I received 51 messages which I compiled into a book, *Wisdom to Consider*. Covering a wide range of topics from compassion, faith, sex, and children, to chakras, working with color, and the divine matrix, I (and others) have found that there is a powerful energy held within its pages. It is not simply the information that is moving. There is an essence that reaches beyond the mind. My sense is that woven within the fabric of each message is a transformative vibration that is transmitted to the reader allowing for changes in consciousness to the degree to which the person is willing and ready.

A little over a year after I stopped receiving these specific writings, the skies opened up again. Although not a poet (I can't recall ever having written one), I was blessed with incredible, powerful poems. They were single and even multiple pages in length, all magically appearing within seconds or a few minutes. Beyond the fact that there were poems falling out of the ethers through my hand and onto a page before me, they even rhymed! Not a requisite to a good poem I know, yet most impressive to a non-poet!

I will admit, it took me a long time to process and integrate what was happening. Years in fact. I found the poems so moving I could not read many of them either to myself or others without shedding tears. I didn't understand why I was being gifted with such beauty, what it all meant, and what I was to do with these treasures from above. Although not something that is in the forefront of my awareness, the experience brought up issues of self-worth. While I think I'm a pretty cool individual (insert smiley face here), I felt a divide between the extraordinary nature of what was being presented to me and my own humanity. I felt a sense of responsibility for doing something with the poems and a sense of loss in not knowing what to do.

There are over 550 poems to date, and while I still do not fully grasp the magnitude and reasons behind my receiving the poetry, there are a few things that that this experience has helped me to more fully understand and reconcile.

First of all, sometimes we don't know why and that's ok. Trying to answer the unanswerable "why" can keep us locked in place. Sometimes it's in our best interest to surrender to the unknown and say, this is just the way it is. This admission frees us up to move forward in our lives.

Secondly, among other ways my soul lovingly communicates directly with my ego/mind through these writings. It is an outright conversation. Undeniable. Real words on paper. Guidance in black and white.

Finally and most importantly, my soul is calling me to more fully embrace the totality of who I am and release all illusory beliefs that are standing in the way of my living my divinity.

This is where you come in. Your soul, too, is communicating with you every day, and the message is the same. Wake up to your true Self! Waste not another moment. There is a depth of love, joy, peace and freedom within you that is waiting for you to remember. Your soul is calling you to come back home. Will you heed the call?

SUGGESTIONS FOR READING
THE SOUL'S CALL TO AWAKENING

The Soul's Call to Awakening is a soulful offering. Through the author's commentary and channeled poetry, it attempts to give a voice to the soul as it reaches out for our attention, wooing us to go within. It guides, encourages and enlightens us to see what is beyond our limited field of vision and understanding to a landscape of possibility where our true destiny awaits. Each chapter is created to reflect a dimension of our spiritual encounter with ourselves on this journey of awakening.

At the end of each section, there are questions and space designed for you to delve deeper and reflect on your current path, if you choose to do so. If you wish to use the reading of this book as a journey for increased awareness and transformation, you may want to use a separate journal to write your answers along with insights, dreams and experiences that may arise. It may now be time for you to enter into a more conscious relationship with your own soul. This may be a beautiful opportunity to get the conversation started in a way that feels more concrete to you. If this is where you find yourself, you can simply sit with your heartfelt intention of becoming more cognizant of this dialogue (which is already happening) without a preconceived notion on how that might occur.

It is suggested that you take your time, creating the internal and external space to allow the words and vibration to move you. Read each poem several times before moving on. The audio version of all of the poems is available to help you connect more deeply. (Please visit **isabelmartinventura.com** under Books and Writings for information on how to access the files).

You may resonate with some poems more than others in which case you may consider re-reading these as you feel called. You may want to journal your impressions; the thoughts, emotions, feelings, physical sensations and memories that come to the surface as you engage with the messages before you. Pay attention not only to the words, phrases and ideas that produce a "positive" response, but also be mindful of anything that creates a strong impulse to dismiss what has been read. These will all be signs lovingly directing you to bring your awareness to places that are calling to be healed and/or awakened.

Then simply become a witness to your everyday life. Observe and make connections. You will be shown through people, situations and your own reactions that which is ready to be brought to the forefront of your awareness and reconciled. When we choose to engage fully and consciously, we begin to realize how the universe organizes itself to meet our intentions. It's amazing what can happen when we're paying attention!

Finally, the poems are presented exactly as they were channeled. Not a word has been changed. Line demarcations are as they were originally written. Only punctuation was added for better readability. This is not meant to be work of analysis, so commentary on the meaning of each poem is intentionally kept to a minimum. Spirit moves beyond the mind, so just set your intention to receive what is in your best interest and allow the words to move you as such. Also, you will note that some poems use the term *her* or *him*. Know that these loving messages are for all and that the divine is free from definitions of any kind.

THE CALL

While veiled in myriad designs, the spiritual journey is the same for us all, to live our divinity while here on earth. Some actively seek the path. Others walk without deeming life spiritual in nature. Regardless, at a certain point there will be heightened pull to connect more deeply with an unknown part of ourselves. This is the soul calling us to awaken.

To some individuals, the call is heard as a whispering that there is more to everyday reality than meets the eye. There is a hunger to discover the mysteries of life, a desire to uncover and experience the potential that fills the heart, and a longing to bring forth the promise of a higher way of being. You may be able to identify these type of seekers as they travel on pilgrimages to holy sites, burn incense, visit temples, churches and other edifices of spiritual intention, meditate, chant, read spiritually-focused materials, seek out healers, gurus and time alone in nature or engage in the occasional (or frequent) downward dog, all in the pursuit of deeper spiritual understanding and enlightenment.

There is also the seeker who may not be aware that he/she is engaged in the process. Everyday life consists of work, cooking, family, friendships and childrearing without a specific focus on a spiritual pursuit. While this type of existence may not seem like an indicator of a spiritual journey, it is the most common practice. You see, we are all on the same ride. We boarded the moment we entered the earth plane. It's just that some of us haven't looked up to see we are all on the same train, while others are enjoying the trip in joyful anticipation of our final destination.

Regardless of where we find ourselves, the journey of awakening usually arises when the individual begins to hear the soul's calling to focus within. It may appear as if out of nowhere as a curiosity or knowing that there is something more. It may be a casual conversation or a book that sparks the inner quest. Sometimes the call comes in the form of a life-altering event, perhaps a death, illness, divorce or a more joyous occasion such as a marriage, birth of a child or the landing of a dream job. In any event, there is an inner pull (or push) urging us to look beyond our circumstance. It is a stirring that says there is something more, and I want or need to find out what it is.

Once we hear the call, we are changed. We may try to deny it or put it on the back burner for a while, but the stirring will inevitably return, seeking our undivided attention.

REMEMBRANCE (III)

Hello.

It's me.

Your delight

to see.

Your now.

Your then.

Your forever

more to

be.

Your soul.

Alive.

Awaiting your

reply

to love

it All

from within

the call.

You are

my love.

The one

I do

desire

to be.

The one
who forever
more replies
to love
alive
within the
here and now.

Hello, will
you
open up
your eye
and see
the me
within the
all there
is?

With love,
your soul
awaiting your
recall.

∞

Remembrance (III) is pretty straightforward. It is a love letter from your faithful friend who has accompanied you across all time and who promises to be with you forever. You are the one and only. Love and delight wait for you. You have forgotten about the relationship, but your soul has not forgotten you. It waits patiently for you to see clearly and remember who you are.

A Love Letter similarly calls the seeker to remembrance. Here we get the sense that the soul longs to unite with its sleeping counterpart. There is a patient, deep, "fervent" love, and we are being told that we are of pure essence. We are wondrous, and the truth of who we are waits for us to live this in our waking hours. The soul, our "one true destiny" shares that it lives "to hear your laughter become mine." In other words, the essential part of who you truly are is present, yearning and waiting for your embrace. It is up to you to see clearly and remember.

When we finally allow this union to occur, we no longer filter our expression. Our divine essence and unfolding in the world are one. And from this place of love, we light the way for others to hear the call as well. We become a living testament to the oneness of life.

A LOVE LETTER

Hello my
wondrous self
that remembers
naught of her
demise.
I live to hear
your laughter
become mine.

In fervent
love
I wait alive,
becoming truth
for you to
write
the moment you
finally see
the call.
Together, we
ignite the
way for
others to
remember, too,

the oneness
that pervades
the one
true call.

Until the day
you know it's
me
within your one
true
destiny,
I wait and
revel in
your essence
pure.

∞

Afternoon was the first poem that I channeled. I have read it many, many times and I still love it. At first, my mind was distracted by the seeming contradiction in tense and perspective as it switches between past and present and first and third person. No other poem does this. I have come to attribute this to a mirroring of our journey between the two realms of the material and the spiritual, and an alluding to the sense that soul and self are not separate, but already one.

In our everyday experience, time and space appear as real. However, when it comes to the world of spirit, these constructs are not present. Since we exist in both worlds, these contradictory inputs can leave us feeling confused. This nature of our existence expressed as the "musings and life" are "entangled and mangled and free to unfold." So basically, we have to be able to see beyond the jumble of the real and illusory to discover the true Self.

But let us not get disheartened. The poem's close gives us hope that beyond the self that can get lost in the labyrinth of life, there is a loving counterpart that sees all and is there encouraging us out of the quagmire. And with a knowing smile at that!

AFTERNOON

In the afternoon of my youth, surrounded

by rivers of eternity, I saw myself.

Looming in a humble dwelling, she

peered through the veil of illusion

to smile.

A smile so familiar, yet long

forgotten. I remembered her.

And in my dream,

one few awakened from, I slept

a joyous taste of life's slumber,

yet knew that this was not

where I am to reside.

It is a foreboding nature, this

juxtaposition of musings and life,

entangled and mangled and free to unfold.

I know, she said

and smiled again

to remind me it was time

to awaken.

∞

Once we can no longer deny the call, there may be times when we feel compelled to explore ways to deepen our understanding of what is happening and what is waiting to be discovered. It may feel as if a greater force takes over driving us to examine life and our understanding of it in ways we never had before. We may not fully understand what we are feeling or what we are longing to discover, but we may find ourselves supported by a mysterious wave that moves us closer to our Self.

I have included *Tick Tock* here for several reasons. Firstly, it creates and holds a rhythm that reflects not only the soul's never-ending call to awaken, but our impetus to find the source of the allure. The words can be perceived as a consistent movement, a march to a destination known and unknown.

Secondly, our journey is an interplay between the spiritual and material, the soul and the ego. As has been mentioned, this intermingling can be disconcerting to our human experience. I see the use of the clock in the poem as a bridge that subtly allows the mind to remain open to receive the message contained within the words. Time is of this plane, yet it is being used as a container for a spiritual dialogue. By creating a sense of time, which is familiar to us, we are put at ease and connected with the integral beating of our divinity which resides below the level of our awareness. *Tick Tock* helps us to connect the illusory with what the soul deems as true reality. Within the comfortable ticking rhythm is the offering that the real clock is the "clock alive," the one "within the heart" which is "aware of all, above all time."

TICK TOCK

tick tock

the clock

awakens my

intention

every day,

to be the

one who

sees beyond

it all.

tick tock

reminds me

that within

this fragile

tale I

tell

resides the

wonder of

time devised.

illusion plays

a role

for life;

to emanate
the light
above, within,
between
and sovereign.

tick tock
tick tock
tick tock
the clock
alive lives
within the
heart,
aware of
all,
above all
time,
announcing your
sweet return
back home.

∞

REFLECTIONS ON MY CALL

1. Have I heard my soul's call to awaken? If so, how does my soul communicate with me, and what is it saying?

   If not, what is the reason for reading this book?

2. What am I feeling that is urging me to seek something beyond my everyday life?

THE PROMISE

The soul holds the promise of the fulfillment of our deepest longings. Love. Freedom. Peace. Joy. Life. Beyond the dream we experience as real is a realm where divine love reigns. This "realm" is not a place, but an awareness. Living this perspective, we are free to be all that we feebly attempt to create. Here we are complete.

JOY

Alive, awake, aware

of All.

I am free.

∞

A Waking Dream reminds us that when we turn off everything outside of ourselves, we begin to hear the musings of our truth. At night, the truth "comes to play." In the silence, in the darkness, we begin to see our light. When we allow ourselves to be consumed by the noise of our quotidian lives, we forget our true essence. We are the somnambulist, the sleepwalker. Seemingly awake, but completely unaware of the walk.

The promise is that when we awaken, all becomes alive. Not because anything has changed, but because our vision is now uncompromised. Our perception is clear, free from illusion. In this state, beyond all constructs and fear is where we find home. Again, it is not a place, but the embrace of our divinity. We move through the world with new eyes and all is love.

A Waking Dream

At night the
truth does come
to play
between the sheets
on which you
lay.

It whispers clearly
to your soul
renewing life as
it unfolds.

You wake and
do remember
naught of
love's caress
within your
mold.

Yet
when you
walk alive
you'll see

the night
and day
alive with
thee.

In every step
you do
partake.
In all
entrancing dreams
you make.

Be free to know
it's all alive
within the
wake of
Love
Divine.

∞

HOME

Remember dear,

your warm

residence

is beyond all

mortar strewn

about.

Past all fortresses

to pastures of

desire

is where your

home is

evergreen.

∞

The final destination on this journey that we all share, beyond a shadow of a doubt, is love. It is the promise and the call.

LOVE ASSURED

You deem yourself

incomplete

to fly above

the oceans

deep.

You steep in

regret

to feel yourself

complete.

Deny no

longer your

only cure.

Love

procured.

Assured.

∞

Your Lover's Cup Runneth Over is the final poem in this section. It's pretty sexy. It is the culmination of the promise of divine union and what I think people search for in love relationships. It is the intimate, passionate embrace of becoming one. In an effort to create what we feel intuitively is possible, we search for romance and passion, being swept off our feet and transported to other dimensions of ecstasy. We want to experience the bliss of divine union, and we analyze the person sitting across from us at the restaurant table to decipher whether this is "the one." That's a lot of pressure to put on another human being. But that doesn't stop us from trying!

We may experience glimpses of connection, through sensations or genuine states of communion. But ultimately, this does not sustain us, for the call to reunite with our inner self remains unanswered. It is a call that only you can heed and satisfy. You are the lover and the beloved. Your longing is to experience this ultimate reunion.

YOUR LOVER'S CUP RUNNETH OVER

In the summer's haze,

the heat awakens

my thirst for you.

I dream unencumbered

by the notion of precious

encounters.

My flame adorns your

begotten sun,

and I am free to

explore beyond all

worlds the truth

that is hidden.

Apparent to none

except my inner

thirst for you.

∞

Reflections on The Promise

1. What is the highest experience you desire to share with another in a romantic relationship? What do you perceive is lacking when you do not have this partnership?

2. Recall a moment when you had an experience of oneness with another person or the place. Bring back the feeling and be with it for a couple of minutes. If you cannot recall any, create one in your imagination. How would you describe what you created in this moment?

THE ADVENTURE OF DISCOVERY

At a certain point along the path, our exchange with our inner self starts becoming more fluid. We begin to hear our internal self more clearly and can decipher and share in the joy of discovering who we are. We see that the journey within is not always the easy choice, but it's where we want to be, and we're ready to dig in and get our hands dirty as we engage in the magic of life.

We may recognize that we haven't got a clue. We do not know where we're going, but we know that we want to be there. We are ready and open to taking chances. Experiencing life. The fact is that at this stage, we have passed the point of no return. There is no other option but to forge ahead in search of our truth, and while our footing may still feel unsteady, we are aware enough to choose the gift of enjoying the adventure.

AWAY TO ME

In a dream
I saw my newfound
friend.
She dreams of great
adventures for me.
She sees me on
high sails,
navigating a rough and
open sea.
And as the winds and
salt adorn my face,
she smiles at the
beginnings of my relationship
with life,
a newfound way of
being.
Unafraid to get my
feet wet,
my hands dirty,
my eyes dry.

And as I sail
along towards the
horizon,
she nods and exclaims
that all is as it should be,
with more than
a few adventures
waiting to be discovered.

∞

REFLECTIONS ON
THE ADVENTURE OF DISCOVERY

1. How have you held yourself back for fear of being hurt? How has this affected your connection with yourself and others?

2. How open are you to being vulnerable? What gifts might you uncover from within yourself and the world if you allowed yourself to be more vulnerable?

THE ILLUSION

While the journey of self-discovery is a wonderful adventure, there will be times that will feel difficult and even overwhelming. At some point, we will undoubtedly come face-to-face with having to re-evaluate long-standing thoughts, beliefs, relationships and ways of being. Life will orchestrate itself in a way that will compel us to question aspects of ourselves and life as we have known it.

These moments are pivotal. They are opportunities to unearth the places within us where we have unknowingly stored untruths. We must find and bring light to the crevices that house and protect the hidden fears that we have created or accepted from the outside world. In order to connect with and live from the core of our divinity, we must shed all else.

Painful situations offer the possibility of dissolving illusions that impede our love from flowing forth. The pain occurs because we become aware of a discrepancy between our true Self and the life we are living. A misalignment comes to the surface, and we are forced to examine what is being reflected before us and make a choice. It is in releasing illusory beliefs that we gain awareness and access to higher levels of wisdom, but this is not always easy for those of us residing in human form.

The realm of the soul is much different to that of the mind, and for most of us the latter is where we tend to reside. As we approach our inner selves with greater fervor, we will invariably be met with an internal resistance. We may find ourselves in a relationship or situation that will force us to rethink what we believe is an integral part of who we are. This is the beginning of the process of dissolving to the Self, a necessary step in realizing our own divinity. And really scary to the ego.

In an attempt to keep the status quo, the mind will kick into high gear and cry STOP! We may find ourselves angry, lost, confused and not understanding why something is happening or seeing the blessings hidden in the experience. Thoughts and belief systems that are familial, cultural or even appear to be part of humanity's collective data base may be challenged. It may feel like a test. You may tell yourself to look for the lesson. But there is no lesson. It is you shedding the part of yourself that is not real. The constructs you were told and took on as the truth. The beliefs of good and bad, right and wrong, life and God. You are releasing what does not serve. At this point, you are shedding your skin in anticipation of the new you. Be gentle with yourself, and just keep walking.

And while life may feel confusing at times, do not be surprised by what your journey may reveal. Your soul lives beyond what your mind would like you to believe. Simply

be open to allow your Self to reveal its infinite, loving song
of truth.

THE MORNING BIRD

I saw in the shadow

of my awakened day

a sparrow

who sung a song of death,

a joyous song.

Do you presume the ramblings of your voice

would prefer life over death?

Yonder you will see

that as the sparrow turns

its head to face the wind,

so too will you to see

again the face of

that from whence you

came into being.

And you will prefer naught.

The night nor day.

The pearl nor oyster.

The depth of the seas

nor the heights of the mountains.

For all are equal.

Neither good nor bad.

Even in life as in death.

So you will know

what it means to be in his beloved's breath

and in his divine moment,
which is one in all eternity.
So when you go
along your way,
pleasure or pain,
see this the same.
And you will
learn to laugh at sorrow
and grieve in joy.

∞

I AM (II)

Beware, my mind

does tell a

tale

to keep me far

from yonder path

that underneath

my blessed feet

does become my

solemn mask.

Alive! My heart

does venture

past all

illusion that

unfolds

to remind

me that

I AM

Above, beneath,

between it

All.

∞

At this point of the journey, when we find ourselves in the midst of unanswerable questions, sensing a newfound way of being with no roadmap in sight, the only unreasonable, reasonable option is to surrender. If you desire to delve deeper within, you must give up trying to figure anything out, especially when it makes no sense to the mind. It is this contradiction that must be embraced in order for it to dissolve, revealing the jewel of still awareness in its wake.

SUBMISSION

In stillness, I
forsake the state
of being still.

In joy, I forbid
my smile to
form.

In essence pure,
I AM
alive.

In flying high,
I humbly
submit to
All.

∞

The greatest illusion is that we are not enough and that we have to figure out how to arrive at our divinity. The truth is that there is no journey. We already are divine. Divinity incarnate. I remember hearing this notion for the first time and having the proverbial aha moment. *Of course there is no journey! How could I have figured otherwise?* How could one possibly travel to be where one already is? How would that make any kind of sense?

Our journey is not the type where one arrives at a destination. It is an experience of dissolving all notion of who I am. What remains is who I AM, and who I AM is already here. Because we are divinity incarnate, spirit in the flesh. We can perceive the intermingling between matter and spirit. When we use language to try to define and understand the dynamic, it can create a mental dissonance. The mind thinks in terms of time and space, so it likes to see a beginning and an end and coins this a journey. But since I AM already here, how can it be defined as such?

The point is you are already glorious, magnificent love. Period.

IN FIELDS IN BLOOM

You see yourself

a little bud

encased in possibility,

but in reality

you are a forest

of daffodils in bloom.

You await with bated breath

for your unfolding,

but you my dear

already have enveloped

the world with your fragrance.

Fear not the hows or whens

or maybe thens.

Be you in bloom

as you were born,

without reproach or normal doom

to account for the blessings

you bring.

Oh beauty within.

Oh morning star.

You shine yet know yet

not how far.

Do not await

a morning dawn

to reunite with
your now belonging.
To thee is given.
To thee fear not.
Do not believe
you've yet to see
the magnificence that
is already Thee.

∞

REFLECTIONS ON THE ILLUSION

1. Have you ever experienced a time when your core beliefs were challenged? If so, how were you changed?

2. What thoughts and emotions come up for you when you consider every aspect of yourself dissolving?

3. How would your world change if you moved through your day with the unwavering knowledge that you are divine love?

SOUL LOVE

As we have seen over and over again, your reunion with your soul is its unwavering desire. In *Soul Love,* we are gifted with seeing the truth of the expansiveness that we already embody. While we stumble in trying to find ourselves, thinking that we need to exert effort in navigating towards the Promise Land, the soul whispers, "fear not". Surrender and be. You are beyond your expectation and imagination. You are the "stars and sights," "the wind behind the sail." You are alive, already the All that is, and it is your own love that patiently waits for you to remember.

A PATIENT LOVE

You stream between the
here and now
longing to believe
that everything is
waiting for your
call.
Yet dear, you are
among the rides of
oceans reaching
towards the shore.
No effort needed
to be free.

You are alive.
You're free to be
the ocean's revelry,
enjoying all the
sights along the way.

Yet if in fear
your quest is to
navigate yourself,
tired will you
be within the
way.

You see you are the
stars and sights,

the witnessing of man
who longs to hear the
call within the Self.
Yet doing so, relinquishing the
truth that's Heaven sent,
the oneness gives way to
love Divine.

Fear not
and Be.

Be free
to sail

amidst the
ocean's course.

Believe you are
the wind behind
the sail.

Alive you stream
in consciousness
awaiting to arrive
to where your
love awaits
for thee.

∞

REFLECTIONS ON SOUL LOVE

1. How do you experience patience within yourself? When are you most willing to wait?

2. What are you putting off pursuing? What are you waiting for? What is the fear?

Soul Guidance

Sometimes we do not know the answers and feel lost. Although all is within us, we are still blind, thinking that there is something to understand. In *Revealed Wonder*, we are reminded that the mind is not where we find relief, but it is the heart that holds the love that soothes. We are urged to be in silence to know what it is we long to discover.

REVEALED WONDER

You see and feel the
sun's delight,
the warmth of life
upon your brow,
yet still you think
there's something else
to know.
Go beyond confusing
thoughts to
where your heart
resides in
love,
then will there be
nothing else
to find.

Beyond your mind
is where you
are.
In silence still,
serenity.
In passion's arms
is where you
do reside.

Breathe deeply to

encounter you,

then all illusions

melt away

revealing that

for which

you long to

know.

∞

As we have seen, when navigating the spiritual path, our first inclination is to go to the mind. Because the mind is accustomed to finding patterns to get a sense of the world, there is a tendency to look to the outside for comparison. In the earnest effort to understand ourselves more deeply, we do the opposite of what will deliver us into wholeness.

In *Perched Awareness*, we are guided to know our uniqueness and understand the misguided manner in which we approach ourselves. No other "can portray the one residing in your skin." As such, it would be a foolish endeavor to look beyond the Self. Only you can know yourself, your fullness, your expansiveness.

PERCHED AWARENESS

Two birds did perch
upon themselves
to see how high their
vision flew
to bend the notion that
exists
between the newness
that is
you.

To see how high the
mountain
climbs,
no need to fall upon
your knees.
Expand the vision
of your eye,
and gaze upon
your only
need.

You see no other
can portray

the one residing

in your skin,

for with the

eyes that

in your head

refuse to see

beyond the

need

that does pervade

your every thought.

So separate the

unity that separates

at every course

when you forget

that you are

me.

Together we do now

reside

within the breast

that's heaven

sent,

so when you perch

upon a branch,

seek only to relate

yourself

to those who share

your life with

you.

No need to

look beyond

yourself,

but glory for the

brethren fool

who looks to

you as does

yourself.

∞

Until the day that we are able to spread our wings and truly fly, *Free* encourages us to live our lives "without recoil." This provides the stepping stone to start being as the soul, unencumbered by fear and judgment. It is fear that creates the cage that surrounds us and judgment the false separation between ourselves and others.

When we move through life without withdrawing from any thought or situation, we embody the neutrality of spirit, embracing all of life. This does not mean that we are paralyzed to act. It means that we are free to be guided by spirit to use our lives to create from the perspective of the heart. With clarity of vision, we relate and reflect connection and contribute to a world where all of life is taken into consideration. When we reject anything, we are limited by the rules of duality and therefore create separation. By embracing all, we embody our divine nature and are able to set ourselves free.

FREE

Between the dark and light

I fly

reminding all of destiny

to be alive and

love

eternally.

But while your eye is

hindered still,

simply be without

recoil

until the day

your wings

unfold at

last.

∞

REFLECTIONS ON SOUL GUIDANCE

1. How freely do you engage in life? In what ways to you hold yourself back from being fully engaged with others?

2. What are the recurrent judgments you make of others? Of yourself? What fears (about yourself and world) are connected to these judgments?

3. How would your experience of life be different if you were free from judgment?

THE LONG ROAD

The earnest pursuit of answering the inner call is not an easy task. After a while, the road will begin to seem long and arduous, and we may even begin to question the point of it all. It can feel like no matter what we do or how hard we try, we fail to experience the transformation that we seek. Regardless, we continue.

We may become weary and tired. At times we must stop to rest, but eventually we rise and go on walking. We know that our vision remains blurry, but we also sense that *only we* can find our way out of the maze of illusion that we have created. Deeper still is the resounding promise of the heavenly repose that waits eagerly for our arrival.

WEATHERED WANDERER

Somewhere between
love and fear
I find myself.
Hovering there I
find repose
and yield to
find my
sacred Self.

When rested, I
shall be released
and dwell again
between my gait
and time.

∞

CLOUDED VISION

Tomorrow comes today

and yesterday is

tomorrow's need.

In between, I gasp

for breath

and look on for

a new sign

of life

amidst the clouds

and smoke that

fog my sight.

∞

BATTERED WINGS

Wounded, I
arose to find
a precious knowing
of my mind.
I am the
only bird to
fly above.
I can connect
with those who
know
Divinity within
the flow,
yet I alone
can call
my wings
to beat
above the
winds of
time.

Battered, I
embrace the
call,
and with

my tune
alive,
I fly again
with eyes on
yonder
field

where flowers bloom
and butterflies
announce the
arrival of my
I
and where I
finally
breathe my
freedom's
ring.

∞

REFLECTIONS ON THE LONG ROAD

1. What have been the times that you have felt most abandoned by life? How were you able to move forward?

2. If you find yourself tired and weary, what is the highest vision that your heart has for you?

TRUTH REVEALED

While it may seem that most of us live with blinders on, struggling and stumbling to try to discover our true nature, *Your Majesty* playfully suggests that our royal lineage is no big secret. The splendor of our divinity is apparent to all of life. While we search to find our truth, life in all its facets is constantly acknowledging our essence. Even the morning knows who we are.

Your Majesty

I spoke with a
mockingbird.
I heard it
clearly say,
"The morning salutes
your majesty."
I turned to see
the way the wind
carried for this
praise, and
surprisingly it
landed right
on me.

I asked, "but
why do you
surmise
I a kingly tale?"
He squawked and
gently flew away.

And as I
turned to walk
away
every blade of
grass saluted
the traces at
my feet.

∞

When we least expect it, our journeying will come to a bend in the road, and we will see a light that had not been previously visible. It may appear in a moment of epiphany or simply show up as a gentle knowing that rises from spirit. What has happened is that the mind has begun to surrender control. When we choose and practice operating from spirit, the mind begins to lose its power over us. It recognizes an unyielding, higher strength and becomes submissive. In recognizing the master, it bows to its rightful position of service. When this occurs, a veil is lifted, allowing our inner light of love to shine through and reveal the treasures we have hidden from ourselves. In this moment, we begin to set ourselves free.

LOVE ENCOUNTERED

Now in darkness
I truly see
the undoing of my
mind.
It calls to me
to engender beginnings,
falsehoods and such.
But there is a crack
in this supposed
armor,
an aberration I did
not account for.
And through this
I see a light
that illuminates all.
I come close to
see a tale long
to be remembered.
This supposed darkness
is the doing of my
eye,
for once I see there
is only light,
I can remember

that which I
have longed for erroneously.
It has been here
all the time.
It has been here
all the time.
It has been here
all the time.

And now I breathe
a slow and moving
breath
that frees me from
the confines of my
mind.
And I am restored.
Finally seeing
my captive is my
host.
My patient is
myself.
And my medicine is
love.

∞

REFLECTIONS ON THE TRUTH REVEALED

1. What gifts or qualities do others say that you possess that you do not fully embrace? To what do you attribute the difference?

2. Can you recall a moment when you had a shift in a core belief or mindset? How did this new perspective create greater freedom within you?

INSPIRATION FOR THE JOURNEY

While we do the work to find our home, we are reminded that it need not be an arduous task, but can be a joyous fulfillment of the promise that is within us. Regardless of the "winds or storms," we are safe within the haven of the heart and until the day we recognize ourselves, we can choose to be fully engaged with all of life.

EMBRACED IN FLIGHT

I wondered how the

robin builds its

nest.

Does it brood and

question life's only

test

to live enamored

with the tale

to tell

and revel in

the building

of a fractured

shell?

Oh, no! It lives

but to fulfill

the burning that

inside

reminds him

how to build

the fortress protecting

all the I.

No matter

winds or storms

that come,
he happily
supplies
the tenderness
for the
heart to
blossom and
reside.
He builds, oh
happily
recoiling not
from flight,
awaiting the promises
residing in the
I.
And then one
day all work
will recognize
itself
and fly away
repeating Divinity's
embrace.

∞

REFLECTIONS ON
INSPIRATION FOR THE JOURNEY

1. What inspires you to continue connecting consciously with your inner being?

2. How might you bring greater joy to your day-to-day life?

3. How is your light inspiring to others?

SURRENDER

Surrender is the only necessary step for becoming one with the Divine. From the human perspective, this is quite scary. After all, if I want to become one with someone or something that means that someone or something is going to die. And this is exactly what will happen. Enlightenment, becoming one with the light, requires the death of the ego.

The ego is a construct of our two-dimensional perspective. In the world of duality, we understand ourselves as a function of how we compare with the world. Male/female, young/old, small/large, alive/dead, this/that. As we have touched upon, our essence is beyond this realm and as such, all else must vanish in order to experience oneness.

To the mind, one plus one cannot equal one, and its primary purpose is to keep you alive. Therefore, as we near our total dissolution, it will not be unusual to find a marked increase in the mind's refusal to change. For the most devoted of seekers, it may be necessary to endure the "dark night of the soul" as the crucible through which stubborn resistance is burned away.

The dark night challenges our deepest beliefs and fears about life, God and our place in the universe. We are helplessly hurled into an abyss of uncertainty and desperation with no hope for resolution. Even Jesus is said to have experienced this trial before his death on the cross, calling out "My God, my God, why hast thou forsaken me?" (Matthew 27:46 (KJV)) The dark night is not a lesson, test or punishment, but rather the mind's last ditch effort to save itself amidst the spirit's heightened longing for union with the Divine. Once concluded, we are cleansed and freer to be reborn into the light of our awakened Self.

Fluttering in the Wind highlights the arduous, yet joyous effort of weathering the passage to awakening and suggests that disappearing is the most precious journey to embark.

FLUTTERING IN THE WIND

I see in the

recesses of beyond

a calling,

a near death experience

waiting to be awakened.

It calls me like

a moth to a flame

and I know that

I, too, will be consumed.

And yet I go

wings in toll.

There is no other

journey I'd rather

undertake,

for although I

know I will soon

disappear,

it is too long

in the making.

I fear not the

removal of me.

I long for this.

It, too, will be

the day that I needed

to compensate for my

meager ways,

but I know that

first I must endure

a small fraction of reality

before I am to become

aware fully of the flame

before the moth.

In the rain,

in the wind,

my wings beleaguer

the call,

and I joyously toil on

to my demise.

∞

REFLECTIONS ON SURRENDER

1. Have you ever lived the "dark night of the soul"? If yes, what was the gift that remained from the experience?

   If not, recall the most difficult experience that you have lived. Depending on our choices, these times provide the opportunity to receive gifts of wisdom and surrender. What thoughts/beliefs did you most struggle with when processing the experience? What if any positive outcome did you realize?

2. Are you aware of a time when you chose to surrender instead of struggling to find answers? How did that decision change your perspective on life?

Awakening

Morning's Glory

My soul awake

does render forth

its love.

It streams through

me to reach

beyond the stars.

It says, I'm here

to live enamored with it all.

Epiphany within

the hands of

morn.

∞

When the day of our awakening arrives, we learn how truly blind we have been and laugh knowing that what we have been searching for has been within us, and in everything, all along. We rise from the dream to see that we are eternal, infinite, divine. All is aware and awake and alive. And love, the only rule.

THE ONLY RULE

I woke up today

to see the light.

The passages of man

unraveled to

reveal the

story

of all time.

The never-ending

search for

my existence

all rolled up into

one desire.

I laughed out

loud at

my reprise,

at fortune staring

back at me,

and I, encumbered by

my eye,

could see nothing

but the dream.

It all aware.

It all alive.

It all within my every breath.

And I so supple and so wise,

yet paralyzed
by eager breadth
of things to see
and steps to take,
of oceans deep
for me to quench
my thirst for
what I longed
to feel,
yet all along
embodied pure.

The I in me.
It all in he.
The essence of
my birth's procure.
To be alive
I longed to be,
when all along
eternity
is the name

upon my
breast,
for all to rest
within me now,

to live and breathe
within my gait
is where salvation
is absolved.

I laugh today
with gentle touch.
I realize my
precious gift.
I am the now
eternal one
that lives amidst
the winds of
time.
Between the
here and
there, I AM.
Before and after
all there is.

This is where
truly I exist,
where one and two
are trinity.
When nothing matters
and is whole.

Where love is
all that does
belong.
Love, the master
and the cure.
Love, the heart's
only rule.

∞

When we understand who we are, we are free to walk our days simply being. We are unencumbered by the fears, beliefs and judgments that previously defined us and orchestrated our life through the choices we made. Now in full awareness, we radiate our light wherever we go and with whomever enters our life. We are love in motion. Divinity fully expressing itself.

I SEE

My senses fly

beyond my mind

to places filled

with love's

delight.

There I radiate

my only truth.

My life, to

be remembered

well

within the

carcass of

my shell

and reunite

the oneness

of the

way

with all

I see,

do and

feel,

with

reality

perceived

as

real.
This I make
my only
call in
life.
I then surmise
it's time
to be
infinity
within
the
me
that
walks
with
love
among
the
All
I
see.

∞

A SACRED WALK

I knew the song
of life.
It rattled through
my brain,
yet I in
strife
forgot the most
exquisite refrain.
Then one day
I appeared
reminding me
of how
to sing the
song within
the corridors
of life.

My heart remembered
all.
Awake, it
sang to me,
and tears ran
down my
face

washing me
in destiny.
I simply now
rely
on the way
the winds
direct,
the tune of
life alive and
I within
its wake.

No course to take.
No path to serve.
No reminiscent
tales to tell.
Simply I within myself
creating life alive.

∞

REFLECTIONS ON AWAKENING

1. Sitting in a quiet setting, close your eyes and take several slow, centering breaths. Ask to be shown how it feels to be aware, awake, alive and radiating divine love.

Who I Am

I AM. The One True Fire. A Blessing. A Flower. The Face of Love. This is who you already are.

ALIVE (V)

I breathe.

I see.

I reach.

I climb.

I still the

hubris inside.

I am.

I'm free.

I still

the night

with love

so deep

it rectifies.

I breathe

alive

the call to

life.

My flight

ignites my

soul to

fly

above all

95

notions

men

surmise

to places

love

does

recognize.

Aware,

I'm cool

to face

the fire.

I wean

myself of

reconciles

that stream

across my

heart's desire

and alive

I AM

THE

ONE

TRUE

FIRE.

∞

A BLESSED ROSE

The flower that is me
lives quietly above
the noise that
surrounds my every day.
She blooms within
the heart
that gives not to
receive
and blesses the
rose with fragrances
of love.

∞

FACE OF LOVE

I tried.
I failed.
I thought I'd be
the one and
only
recipe,
yet now I see
I do not
need
to roll the
dice to
find the
me I
seek.
Here I AM,
awaiting pure
for me to
see I
the allure,
do reside in
time and
space
to be
the semblance
of the
face of
love.

∞

REFLECTIONS ON WHO I AM

1. The Divine expresses its many qualities through many manifestations, you being one of these. Without giving it too much mental energy, write down the divine qualities that come to life through you?

The Soul's Call for Humanity

While the soul's calling feels personal, it rings true for the whole of humanity. As our individual level of consciousness rises, so too does that of the human collective. As you awaken, you awaken the world.

DAWN DELIVERED

Let's play
today
at this one
great game.
Let's see the
nations rule
with love
abundant,
hearts aflame,
let's see salvation
rule.
Be free to know
that joy
abounds amidst
the skies above
and that your
passage to this
plane

is as it was
ordained.
To know within
your heart
this truth
transforms all
into love.
The slave enamored
with his host.
The priest with
kingdom come.
To be one
with this joyous
dance,
your choice is
the
revenge to all
the fears that
dwell among
the mirroring of
men
who fail to see
within themselves
the calling and

the light.
You see it
all is waiting
for
your reunion
with the I.
That is where
joyous symphonies
aligned with his
desire
do seek to revel
in your
knowledge of
hearts that
set afire
the remnants of
precocious thoughts
awaiting to expire.
The heart knows
how and where
and when.
Surrender to its
choir
of love adorned,
of nations proved

by his salvation

song.

Release the light

for all to

see

this is the

Grand New Dawn.

∞

ABOUT THE AUTHOR

Isabel Martin-Ventura is an energy healing practitioner, teacher, author and life coach, who helps individuals connect with themselves and the deeper, spiritual nature of life.

She began practicing energy healing in 1997 and has been channeling the written word since 2009. Channeled works include *Wisdom to Consider*, a compilation of 51 messages speaking to the human condition and its connection to the Divine, as well as hundreds of spiritually inspired poems. The poetry is a reflection of the soul's call reminding us of our divinity and heralding us to live who we are - love in the now.

Isabel has supported hundreds of individuals seeking healing and guidance through spiritually focused, self-empowerment workshops, retreats and one-on-one sessions in her private practice. She holds a psychology degree from New York University, has studied a variety of complementary healing techniques in the U.S. and abroad, and has professional experience in media and education.

Please visit **isabelmartinventura.com** for inquiries and information on private sessions and events.